Falco

Walking with God and a Dog

by

Andy Falco Jimenez

Walking with God and a Dog Video

Published by Tactical Productions, Brea, CA

All Scripture quotations taken from the New International Version, the New Living Translation, and the Complete Jewish Bible

Picture on cover was taken at the Los Angeles riots in 1992. Falco and Andy were assigned to protect the Fire Fighters from Anaheim as they both protected lives and property.

The author took the picture of dog running. This picture is of Police K9 Eddy from Indio Police Department.

www.FalcoK9Academy.com

Dedication Page

To my Police Dog, Falco von Aramis. I am forever indebted to you and thank you for teaching me so much about being a Christian and a leader.

To my wife Beth and all my children: Courtney, Kelly, Constance and Rhett. Your love, forgiveness and encouragement have fueled me and kept me motivated during the years leading up to this book.

To Paul Kraemer, the man who gave me the push, encouragement, love and respect that I needed at the perfect time. I will always remember Paul as the man who truly led me to God, Jesus Christ and the Holy Spirit.

To Pastor Mathew Cork and all the leaders and congregation at Friends Church Yorba Linda. This place has really allowed me to

www.FalcoK9Academy.com

grow in my faith. They made a broken and lost soul feel comfortable and welcome. Mathew's leadership of the church and PERFECT messages always spoke to me on a personal level.

To Victoria Kovacs, our editor and "Bible fact finder" who dedicated herself to this project and made it better than I could have ever imagined. Thank you!

And last and most importantly, Neil Saavadra, the Producer of "The Jesus Christ Show". And even though he has no idea who I am, his radio show came to me at a perfect time when I was lost and looking for answers. I turned on KFI Radio (Los Angeles) on a Sunday morning and heard a man who introduced himself as "Jesus Christ your holy host". After I got past the self talk of *"Really… can he do that?"* I began to listen (and haven't stopped), and I learned more about God's grace, love and forgiveness than any other place or person up to that time. The show truly opened my mind and allowed me to grow in my faith. I can't say enough about how important this show was to me as a Christian.

Contents

Introduction

For he will order his angels
to protect you wherever you go.
— Psalm 91:11 NLT

In 1992, Falco, my partner and police dog, and I were working patrol in the city of Anaheim. While detaining a group of gang members (with Falco's presence used to motivate them to cooperate), I heard a call over the radio about a shooting with two suspects seen fleeing the scene. They left the victim lying in the street riddled with several gun shot wounds.

An hour later I was finally able to respond to the call.

I wanted to see how Falco's senses might be used to help

solve the crime. The K9 trainer told us that, "Dogs can't track. It's a myth; they really can't." Yet I also heard about the miraculous finds handlers had made with their "tracking" dogs. Was it just a myth? I soon found out that tracking was in fact possible and Falco was particularly good at it.

When we arrived on the scene, I didn't see any obvious physical evidence, which would lead us to the suspects, but I did know Falco was trained to locate any evidence such as guns, knives, or keys which carried the suspect's scent. If the suspects had thrown the gun they used in the shooting into a nearby bush, Falco would smell the human scent and lead me to it.

When I gave Falco the command to search for such articles, he started sniffing the ground at the very spot where one of the suspects had stepped as he fled the scene. Holding onto Falco's leash, he suddenly took off through the front yards of the neighborhood. He pulled on the leash like I had not felt before as I jogged behind him. While I was not trained in the art of tracking, Falco had his head down and was intent on following the scent he had picked up. I was just along for the ride.

While running through the fourth front yard, I asked a resident standing there if he had seen two subjects run that way in the past hour or so. "No," he replied, "but I heard what sounded like a couple guys run down the alley about forty-five minutes ago. It was right after I heard a gunshot over by State College."

During our exchange, Falco never lifted his head and continued to follow the scent. He suddenly turned north between two houses but was stopped by a cinderblock wall dividing the front yard of the homes from the alley at the rear. Falco sniffed the wall and put his paws on it, telling me he wanted to go over. There was a gate just to the right so we went through it.

When we entered the alley, his pull became stronger and his breathing more rapid. My heart was pounding as I drew my weapon. It was time to call for a back up, but I hesitated. It was supposedly impossible for Falco to do what I thought he was doing. But what if he *was* following the tracks of two armed and dangerous suspects?

While I wasted time arguing with myself, Falco led me to a side door of a garage. He began to whine and bark at the door, which stood ajar. I was convinced it was possible he had led me to the felony suspects so I got my best friend, Officer Chuck Alvarado, on the radio and told him what I had. He immediately responded to my location and I showed him the door and told him how Falco led me there. We decided to call for a sergeant and further assistance.

A perimeter was established around the house and the residents evacuated from the home. Chuck and I were given the okay to search the garage with the help of Falco. I pushed open the door with my foot but it only opened half way. I saw a lot of boxes and junk inside, so I was not surprised the door didn't open all the way. I shined my flashlight through the doorway and there lay one subject on the garage floor. He appeared to be asleep, but as I took a closer look, I saw him breathing heavily as if he were scared or just finished running a mile.

I had my eyes, gun, and light trained on the suspect with Chuck over my shoulder doing the same. "I need you to walk toward my voice with your hands up," I ordered him but got no response. I continued to yell at the suspect and although he'd fidget, he refused to cooperate.

I realized I hadn't heard a sound from Falco who would normally be barking and growling at a suspect. I assumed he couldn't see the suspect and if I could get him to bark maybe the suspect would comply. I was sure Chuck had the suspect covered, so I glanced down to see what Falco was doing. He struggled to get around the half open door. Because he hadn't let me down before, I released more leash and allowed him to go around the door. With a loud, guttural growl, he pulled back as if he was dragging something. It was a human leg in his mouth.

"There's someone behind the door!" I told Chuck. "Come out from behind the door with your hands up!" I ordered while I kept another eye on the subject on the floor.

"Okay, I'm coming out. Please tell the dog to let go," said the second suspect. At the same moment something metallic hit the ground. The suspect on the ground suddenly became wide awake and complied with our commands. Both were taken into custody.

Chuck and I went into the garage to ensure there were no other suspects hiding inside. I found the handgun used in the shooting on State College Boulevard; that was what made the metallic sound. Apparently, the suspects wanted to get us to enter the garage with the noncompliance of Suspect #1. I'm sure Suspect #2's job was to shoot if we did.

Falco saved our lives that day doing what the experts said was impossible. If it wasn't for his God-given canine senses, I wouldn't have lived to see my children grow up or retire from the police force to start my own dog training academy.

Dogs have so much to teach us if we will only listen to them.

God has so much to teach us if we will only listen to Him.

This book is about listening to both.

Some people have a hard time believing God exists. Others think He's up there but doesn't speak to them. Still others view God as a hard taskmaster who will punish them for the least infraction like an impatient owner who hits or kicks a dog. With hindsight I realize God speaks to us all the time but we don't always recognize it.

The time I spent with Falco was filled with circumstances which coincided with God and His messages in the Bible and through Jesus Christ. He spoke to me through my dog's hard work and devotion about love, faith, trust, forgiveness—things which help you become a better person, things which help you to "'Love the Lord your God with all your heart and with all your soul and with all your strength and with all your mind'; and, 'Love your neighbor as yourself'" (Luke 10:27 NIV). But I missed it.

This book is to help you not miss it. Its goal is to help you in your walk with God as you walk with your dog. I learned many spiritual lessons working alongside my canine partner. I learn them still today as I train people and their pet dogs. Those lessons are presented here. Think of it as a spiritual dog owner training manual which will guide you to be more like Jesus. You'll see how your dog is a follower of you, its master, just as you are a follower of *The* Master.

This book will also show you how to live with, train, and care for your dog from a Biblical perspective. Yes, there is a Biblical perspective for dog training (cats I can't help you with except to say call a priest) and it has a lot to do with consistency and respect. I can't count how many times I've listened to a sermon about walking with God and thought, "That's what I tell my students in dog obedience training class."

Want to hear some great news? God, the ultimate Trainer, is on your side. He wants you to be the best you can be, using your abilities to their utmost and following Him with steadfast devotion. Doesn't it reason that He will do everything to help you in your spiritual walk? It requires training for obedience.

Are you ready to train? Let's get started.

Falco K9 Academy

1-Forgiveness

Even if that person wrongs you seven times a day and each time turns again and asks forgiveness, you must forgive.
- Luke 17:4 NLT

Forgiveness is not easy to practice but it's essential for a healthy outlook, spirit, and body. Jesus was beaten and tortured yet forgave those who did it. As humans, it's hard to believe that *anyone* can forgive someone who'd do something like that to us or someone we loved. But I know it's possible.

www.FalcoK9Academy.com

Police dog training does not have to be brutal to be effective. Unfortunately, some police dog trainers believe it does, just like the one we used to use at the Anaheim Police Department. As a handler I was lead to believe this was the only way to train police dogs. Motivational training was not an option. Back then, we beat and hit the dogs with reed sticks, choked them with sharpened pinch collars, and shocked them with tasers and cattle prods. The purpose was to cause the dog to fear making a mistake and essentially fear its handler (they called it respect), yet in truth it was purely inhumane treatment due the vendor's (contract trainer to the police department) laziness and stupidity.

That was back in the late 1980s. The very same vendor is still brutalizing dogs today and does it to the majority of the police dogs in the U.S.; so do several other trainers. Some even use food as a training method and starve dogs for days at a time until they get the result they want. It is a tragedy.

Yet after all the hitting and choking and prodding, the dogs still came to us when we called, wagged their tails when they saw us, worked for us in the streets, and saved our lives. Dogs are great at forgiving those they love and respect.

On that faithful night, Falco chose to forgive all that the trainers and I had done to him. He put it aside and chose love for me and gave me life. He also forgave Chuck. Chuck had been preparing to be a K9 handler and in doing so he'd play the role of the bad guy by putting on the padded equipment. He was told *on my command* to hit Falco with a reed stick, causing him pain if he didn't comply with my commands.

Dogs have a lot to teach humans about forgiveness. Sometimes dogs can appear so carefree and oblivious to the fact that they just got yelled at for chewing up a new pair of expensive leather shoes or for sneaking a steak off a plate when its owner's back was turned. A smile, a kind word, a pat on the head, and they're good to go. Just like how God is referred to numerous times in the Bible, they are, "slow to anger, abounding in love and faithfulness."

Wouldn't it be nice to be that free? Instead, we nurse old wounds, harbor resentment, and keep reliving the moment of injury. We want justice (acknowledgement that we are right); we want a sincere (preferably groveling) apology; we want to not feel violated. We want to be free of the issue.

The only way to freedom is to forgive.

Paws to Pray:
Lord, help me to forgive people not just because You say I should and not just because I've been forgiven, but because in letting go of my "right" to hold a grudge, I am freed to love You and others more.

Paws for Dogs:
Sometimes we're quicker to get angry with those we love than with strangers. Our dogs are often the recipients of that anger and frustration. I once slammed the door of my patrol car on Falco's tail after an unsuccessful narcotics search. I apologized all the way home. I was completely out of line in taking out my anger on my dog. Don't forget to verbally and physically apologize to your dog and ask for its forgiveness. It will make a difference in both your and your dog's life.

Is my dog trainable?

www.FalcoK9Academy.com

2-Obedience

*And this is love: that we walk
in obedience to his commands
- 2 John 1:6 NIV*

Obeying God isn't always easy because of our egos, fears, and doubts. Sometimes He gently nudges us to do a particular thing while at other times He's blunt and firm about the direction He wants us to take—not for the sake of being harsh, but because it's vital that we obey because our life or someone else's life is at stake. By obeying, we are rewarded with joy and peace when we see others blessed—all because we allowed ourselves to be used by God.

Obedience takes training. When I joined the K9 unit I didn't agree with the brutal methods used to train the dogs into obedience, nor the blatant abuse of them, which had nothing to do with shaping them into police and detection dogs and everything to do with human ignorance.

Andy and Falco at the 1992 Redondo Beach
Police K9 Trials

One day during training I allowed my dog Falco to be chained to a pole and beaten. It wasn't to make him tougher or prepare him for the street. It was just abuse, senseless and unnecessary. Afterward, Falco greeted me, loving as ever. He knew I watched him being struck and bruised and

www.FalcoK9Academy.com

did nothing to stop it, yet he never flinched from obeying me despite my betrayal.

I was ashamed.

That's when I went to the administration of Anaheim Police Department and demanded a change. I told them the K9 unit could not return to that training facility. They saw the sincerity in my face and my words. And do you know what? We never returned. No department had ever done that but others would soon follow.

After leaving there, I founded a new way of training dogs based on rewards, mutual respect, and without beating dogs within an inch of their lives. My intention was to teach handlers how to train dogs through a clear understanding between the dog, handler, and decoy. Obedience would be gained through respect and not with force, fear, or pain. I outlawed sharpened pinch collars, tasers, cattle prods, and sticks to hit the dogs. Instead, we used a rewards-based system when possible and kept humane corrections to a minimum. Thanks to mentors like Billy Nott, Bob Wright, Mark Ficcadenti and Steve Wright. Who were leaders (and still are) in the police K9 world and in training dogs with respect and love.

Just as I suspected, this method works masterfully.

Just like God, we don't need to beat dogs or others into submission. God does not beat His children into submission. "Take my yoke upon you, let me teach you, because I am gentle and humble at heart, and you will find rest for your souls," Jesus says through His Word. The gentle hand and humble heart gets better results (obedience or "rest for your souls") than cruelty.

Aren't you glad we have such a loving and patient God?

Paws to Pray:
Lord, help me to love you by obeying You and help me to show others the same grace You show me as they learn to obey.

Paws for Dogs:
To teach your dog that you are in charge and a leader to be respected, make sure your dog/s sit and wait while you place their food on the ground. The dog must wait for you to stand and then look you in the eye before they are given the "okay" to eat. As the dog learns to sit, wait, and look for the signal, make sure to vary the amount of time the dog needs to hold this position, but be reasonable.

3-Why, God?

Why, O LORD, do you stand far off?
Why do you hide yourself
in times of trouble?
– Psalm 10:1 NIV

There are many unanswered questions we have as followers of God. Why is there war? Why are so many children abused and molested? Why do bad things happen to good people? These "whys" hit everyone at some point. They were the most challenging of all the issues I had with religion when I was a younger man. They were the reason I argued against God and Jesus—"If there was a God, these things wouldn't happen."

As a police officer I saw the atrocities of mankind which formulated those "whys." There was one week in particular while on K9 patrol in Anaheim when a series of events happened which had me questioning God's existence.

The first was a call of domestic violence. Neighbors heard a man cursing at a woman who was screaming for her life. Upon arrival with my backup officers, I forced open the door of the apartment because we didn't hear a response from inside, only the sound of a small child crying. We found the body of a woman lying in the middle of the family room. Twenty-two stab wounds showed through her blood-soaked clothing and on the bare skin of her arms. A girl just old enough to speak straddled her mother, pulling on her clothing and pleading, "Wake up!" The suspect was gone.

A few days later, a call came out about a car on fire at an apartment complex only a couple blocks away from where I was parked in my vehicle catching up on some reports. I put my things away so I could drive to the complex but didn't rush because, after all, this was a fire call, not a police call, and it was just a car. Then the dispatcher made a second broadcast: "There may be a baby inside the car." I floored the accelerator, turned on my lights and siren, and screeched into the apartment complex, nearly crashing into the fully engulfed vehicle. I tried to break the windows but the flames and heat were too intense and onlookers pulled me away. The two-year-old strapped in the car seat died. Later, the mother admitted to setting the car on fire on purpose with her daughter inside because her boyfriend didn't like the girl.

If that wasn't enough, a couple days later I was in pursuit of a suspect who violated a restraining order. The suspect spun out on the 91 Riverside Freeway and I ended up bumper to bumper with his truck. When I shined the spotlight into the cab, I saw the suspect pointing a 44 Magnum under his chin. From behind my car I pleaded with him to put down the gun and come out, but instead he explained what had happened. Distraught over his life, he said he, "only wanted to see his kids." He told me his ex-wife was remarrying and was keeping his kids from him and he was afraid of losing them. He was clearly contemplating pulling the trigger.

The sergeant on scene was concerned about the traffic jam this stop would create since it was close to the start of morning rush hour. He ordered me to move my patrol car back to clear the lane and in hope the suspect would put down the gun and come out of the truck. I'd been talking to this man for almost two hours and I knew the only thing keeping him from pulling the trigger was my close proximity. The sergeant again ordered me to move my car, so reluctantly I did. As I put the car in reverse with my spotlight still shining on the suspect, he pulled the trigger as I watched.

"Why, God?"

Why would a loving God allow these things to happen? Why didn't He protect the woman who got stabbed? Why didn't He make me act quicker to get to the burning vehicle sooner? Why did He allow the sergeant to give the order to move my patrol car? The canned responses didn't work: "It's God's greater plan," or "God acts in mysterious ways." For me, those answers weren't good enough.

I was so angry at God that I determined to be agnostic and even considered atheism. If God wasn't going to answer my questions, then I wasn't going to have anything to do with Him.

Now, Falco was with me on every one of these calls. He listened when I'd ask, "Why?" He'd comfort me with his head on my shoulder; he'd comfort me when I'd cry. He was there on every call when I needed him to protect me and when I needed him to carry me through a call, he would. Falco gave me strength and confidence when I felt weak and vulnerable. And he was there when I felt alone and abandoned.

His answers were available—I just wasn't open and willing to hear them. God gives humanity free will, and while He does everything to encourage people to do the right thing, we are free to ignore Him. Just as our pets aren't puppets, we aren't puppets.

"Never will I leave you; never will I forsake you." (Hebrews 13:5). God was there with His arms open wide, waiting for me to run into them, to give Him my pain and anger. He used Falco to comfort me—I just didn't see it. If God can make a donkey rebuke a prophet (Numbers 22:28 & 30) and the weather do His bidding (Psalm 148:8), then He can use a police dog to console a weary cop.

Paws to Pray:
God, help me to quiet my mind and soul to hear Your answers to my questions and to remember they aren't always what I expect them to be.

Paws for Dogs:

The most important step in the Falco K9 Academy training system is the "sit, still, stationary, and quite behavior." Everything we do afterward starts from this position. If you can't get your dog to sit, be still, and stationary without barking or whining, it will be hard to get your dog to become obedient in other areas. Work on this today and then increase the stimulation of your dog by doing it on walks or at a park.

4-Mercy

*He does not treat us as our sins deserve
or repay us according to our iniquities.
    – Psalm 103:10 NIV*

It's easy to get upset when hearing about suspects who get away with crimes. We think how unfair the justice system is to allow them to get off scot-free and wish this was the Old West where you took the law into your own hands. "An eye for an eye" makes us feel much better about the most heinous crimes because then we feel justice has been served. Yet as angry as we get about people not "getting what they deserve," it's humbling to remember that as sinners redeemed by the Blood of Jesus, we don't get what we deserve. Because of Jesus dying on the cross to pay the penalty for sin, we've been shown great mercy no matter what sins we've committed.

Falco had an instinct for "eye for an eye" justice, which he dispensed swiftly. Part of a K9's job is to bite a suspect when necessary. This applies only to dangerous suspects who flee, pose a danger to someone's life, or actively resist arrest. Although it's not law enforcement's job to punish suspects, just catch and arrest them, Falco missed that memo. Without fail, when Falco was tasked with biting suspects to allow us to "Catch and Arrest" them, the seriousness of the injuries from his bite were directly related to the crime. For example, a bite to an auto thief caused minor punctures and some redness, while a homicide suspect ended up with torn flesh and exposed tissue which required hours of surgery to repair. The only exception to this rule was after a wild car chase when Falco wasn't able to keep steady in the back of the patrol car and got bounced around. In those cases he came out of the car *very* upset and took out his foul mood on any level of suspect.

Most of our daily lives aren't spent facing criminals who wrong us but we do face strangers, employers, coworkers, family, and friends who we feel have treated us unfairly or sinned against us. We want justice (or vengeance, more likely) concerning these situations, but Jesus says to act in the opposite way from an "eye for an eye" mentality:

> You have heard that it was said, 'Eye for eye, and tooth for tooth.' But I tell you, do not resist an evil person. If someone strikes you on the right cheek, turn to him the other also. And if someone wants to sue you and take your tunic, let him have your cloak as well. If someone forces you to go one mile, go with him two miles.
> Give to the one who asks you, and do not turn away from the one who wants to borrow from you. You have heard that it was said, 'Love your neighbor and hate your enemy.' But I tell you: Love your enemies and pray for those who persecute you. (Matthew 5:38-44 NIV)

Ouch. Instead of getting back at people, Jesus wants us to show mercy. Instead of administering a bite of encouragement to get others to do the right thing as Falco was trained to do, the best thing for us to do is . . . let them get away with what they've done? Let them strike us again? Give them more than what they're suing us for? Go the extra mile? Give when you don't want to? *Love* our enemies and *pray* for them?

"But God," we protest, "Why?!" Because by not resorting to an eye for an eye but choosing mercy, we show we are children of God. We are different, so we must act differently "that you may be sons of your Father in heaven . . . . Be perfect, therefore, as your heavenly Father is perfect." (Matthew 5:45 & 48 NIV)

Perfection is not an easy standard to aspire to but God calls us to it each and every day. And with as much mercy as He shows us ("His mercies never cease. . . . his mercies begin afresh each morning" Lamentations 3:22-23 NLT), we *can* walk in mercy toward others.

Paws to Pray:
Lord, help me to love and pray for those I want to bite. Amen.

Paws for Dogs:
Make sure you aren't causing human aggression in your dog by signaling to it that you're concerned by the presence of a stranger. One of the ways this manifests is by tightening your pull on the leash or wrapping it around your hand when you're on a walk and see someone coming. The dog will get the impression you're scared of the person and by these actions will bark, growl, or lunge at them out of protection and/or fear.

Human Aggression

5-Social Networking

If one person falls down, the other can reach out and help. But someone who falls alone is in real trouble.
- Ecclesiastes 4:10 NLT

Maintaining a relationship with God is like any other relationship; it takes face-to-face time to stay connected. There are times when you talk (pray) and times to be quiet so you can hear what He has to say through reading the Bible or that still small voice in your spirit. While you can't Facebook friend God, you still can have social interaction with Him.

Your dog is a social being. It needs and wants social interaction. Without it, your dog will grow bored and develop bad habits in an effort to find stimulation. The worst thing you can do to your dog is ignore it or reduce your contact with it to feeding and watering and the occasional encounter when you have to mow the back yard or yell at it for destroying something in its effort to alleviate boredom.

Charlie is a long-haired terrier mutt whose owner kept him in his kennel fourteen hours a day. Alone all day long, Charlie was prescribed "doggie Prozac" to calm him down because of "separation anxiety." Of course, anyone with a lick of common sense could see that Charlie wasn't a problem dog. He was being held prisoner and was understimulated. His owner eventually gave him to a shelter which fostered him out to a family with two young boys who loved dogs and a nice backyard to run around in. They adopted him. Charlie now brings much joy to this family. He's a happy dog because they show him that he's wanted.

When you spend time with your dog, demonstrate that you *want* to be with it. Pet it, talk to it, throw a ball for it to fetch, play tug-of-war with a toy. Dogs are masters at reading body language and will quickly detect your anger, annoyance, or reluctance to interact with it.

It's easy to become frustrated by the daily responsibilities which come with owning a dog and forget why you wanted a dog in the first place. When that happens, think back to the reasons which led you to welcome this living, breathing animal into your home. Was it companionship for you or your kids? Was it for home security? Then ask yourself how you felt when this four-legged friend first entered your life. Were you excited? Did you smile and laugh a lot? Were you more patient with its mistakes and mishaps?

Once you reclaim those positive thoughts, restart your relationship with your pet by working on the difficulties which have arisen. Spend a little extra time doing those things you like to do with your dog. By doing so, you'll become a leader for your dog and will look at it with hope, love, and respect, just as it will look to you with respect.

If you find your spiritual life has become dry and stale from lack of social interaction with God, spend a little extra time doing the things you like to do with God: read your Bible, listen to worship music, walk your dog while praying, journal your thoughts. By doing so, you will regain hope, love, and respect for God.

Paws to Pray:
Jesus, help me take time each day to draw closer to You because doing so will help me love and respect You and Your Word more.

Paws for Dogs:
If you're feeling down, spend time with your dog. Talk to your dog and tell it exactly how you feel—dogs are great listeners.

www.FalcoK9Academy.com

Ninety-five percent of dog owners agree that spending time with their dog lifts their spirits. Ninety-two percent say their dog helps them enjoy the simple pleasures in life. Ninety-one percent say their dog makes their lives more fulfilling.

Dog Aggression

6-Facing the Giants

For this is ADONAI's battle,
and he will hand you over to us.
- 1 Samuel 17:47 CJB

The Bible refers to giants multiple times, the most famous being Goliath, the Philistine giant whom David killed. Goliath stood at 9'9" and wore bronze armor plate weighing one hundred and twenty pounds. He carried a spear with an iron spearhead weighing fifteen pounds. None of the soldiers of Israel wanted to mess with him. David, on the other hand, was a lyre-playing shepherd who had killed lions and bears, though he was still called a "boy" and had just been severely scolded by his oldest brother for asking too many questions. His weapon? A sling with five stones. As the story goes, young David defeated Goliath by slinging a stone into his forehead and then cutting off his head with a sword. Since then, Goliath has lived on as a symbol of great odds to overcome.

At 5'10 and one hundred and eighty-five pounds during my career as a policeman, I wasn't small but there were a number of suspects who were larger and more powerful than me. This was never more apparent than during a shoplifting call I answered with my friend Chuck Alvarado. The suspect was described as being 6'7, three hundred pounds, and had "a pint of Jack Daniels in his pants." As Chuck and I got out of our patrol cars, this Goliath exited the supermarket and saw us. I took a deep breath, gulped, and in my most commanding voice ordered him to come to me. He wasn't happy about us disrupting his plans for a one-person party and informed us that he wasn't going to be arrested and he definitely wasn't going to jail. After some negotiating, we talked him into allowing us to pat him down for weapons, but he made it clear he wasn't going to allow us to put handcuffs on him.

While we were talking with him, I had Falco come out of the car via a remote door opener to get a tactical advantage. I commanded Falco to "down" (but be ready) at the bumper of my patrol car (you can see where this is going). As Falco and I acted as cover officers, we had the suspect turn with his back to us as Chuck approached him from behind. Even with the suspect's legs spread and his hands on his head, Chuck had to stand on his tip toes to reach his hands. I knew if the suspect moved or resisted, Chuck would bail out and we'd go to Plan B. As suspected, the suspect spun around and Chuck bailed but he was still able to push Chuck several feet backward. At the same moment, Falco leapt toward the suspect and bit him on the forearm. Normally, Falco didn't bite petty theft suspects but because he assaulted Chuck this was now an assault on a police officer.

As Falco was biting his arm, the suspect punched him. Falco took two good punches to his head before releasing his bite, but he did so not to flee but to get a more effective bite on the giant's shin. When Falco's teeth sank into his leg, the suspect screamed and fell to the ground. He begged to have Falco taken off and agreed to be handcuffed.

Falco, weighing about seventy-five pounds and standing a little over two feet high at the shoulders, did what two grown men with a combined weight of over three hundred pounds couldn't do. Falco's chops had a biting force of over two hundred pounds and with this "weapon"

FALCO – Walking with God and a Dog

toppled a giant—and possibly saved Chuck and me from injury.

We all face giants at one time in our lives or another. Whether it's sickness or incredible odds or debt or disaster, that giant shows up to challenge our faith and freeze us in fear. How will we ever defeat something so *huge*? Yet we must remember God is bigger than any giant. Even when our "weapons" (i.e. our faith, talents, and abilities) don't seem like much compared to the giant's weapons, they are God-given and will be used by Him to take down the enemy. Like David and his sling and stones, or Falco and his fangs, we may not *seem* like the biggest or most qualified to fight, but we must remember the battle is the Lord's. All we have to do is stand up for what is right, employ our weapons, and watch the giant fall.

Paws to Pray:
Father, when I face giants, help me to remember how big You are and not focus on how big they are.

Paws for Dogs:
Your dog should learn the only way to get petted is by having its four paws on the ground, especially with breeds like boxers which love to jump up and "spar" with their

owners. Although you may not mind the dog jumping up on your body and licking your face, a guest or visitor may not like it. Teaching your dog manners is teaching them to respect you, friends, and family.

7-Grrrace

For his unfailing love toward those who fear him is as great as the height of the heavens above the earth.
- Psalm 103:11 NLT

God forgives us no matter what. His grace is irrational. No matter how often or hard we fall, He is there to pick us up. Humans are not so faithful or "grace-full." We find fault with God when He fails to live up to our expectations. We accuse Him of not being there for us when we need Him most. We blame Him for not stopping us when we make bad decisions and exercise our free will (even though we deliberately ignore His nudges and lack of peace in our hearts concerning those decisions).

www.FalcoK9Academy.com

We also like to find fault with our dogs when they fail to live up to our expectations. They're "stupid," "untrainable," or we blame the breed. We sometimes over-punish the dogs (which they don't understand and don't make the connection between the infraction and the punishment). Sometimes we even give them up to a shelter so we don't have to deal with them any longer.

As a police K9, Falco wasn't allowed a lot of room for error. He was trained in strict obedience and I held him to that standard. However, while responding to a "Burglary in Progress Call" one night, Falco tested my patience. After an hour of searching within an established perimeter for the suspect, I gave Falco a break. Searching can be very tiring for a dog due to the amount of area covered and the number of distractions it has to overcome, such as other dogs (including females in heat), small critters, cats, and trash. I commanded him to lay down while I spoke with Officer Mark Irwin about meaningless stuff. To my annoyance, Falco crawled and edged toward a row of bushes. Because I demanded obedience and discipline I told Falco "No" and commanded him to stay in his down position. He wasn't allowed to go pee unless on my command. I thought, *How dare he disturb me?* Seconds later, Falco again crawled and pulled on the leash toward the bushes. I shined my flashlight at them but because they were so small I was sure no one could hide in them. I was convinced Falco only wanted to pee. Even though I was miffed that he wanted to urinate on my time, I gave him the "take a break" command and continued talking with Mark. Falco ran to the bushes as if he had not peed in hours and we heard, "Okay, I give up! Get the dog off of me. I give up." I turned to see Falco pulling a very thin, short male suspect out of the bushes.

"Good boy, good boy, Falco," I said with sheepish relief. Here I had assumed Falco was being disobedient and I reluctantly granted him grace, when all along he knew what Mark and I did not. We had a nervous laugh about it because for ten minutes we had been standing fifteen feet away from the suspect. Thank God he didn't have a gun. Thank God that even on a break Falco was still on the job.

God never gives up—nor should you. All dogs are capable of good behavior. *You* must be a good leader to help them understand the rules of *your* world. If you do this with love and respect while using proper discipline mixed with praise (reward), you will have an obedient follower. Just like a human, your dog will fail (sin) or do something, which seems out of character and incomprehensible. Just like God, you must be there to pick it up, love it, and give it direction to help it not repeat the failure. You must also extend grace to decipher its actions, because a dog always does things with a purpose. Let us be slow to anger and quick to extend grace and understanding both to dogs and humans.

Paws to Pray:
Thank You, Father, for never giving up on me.

Paws for Dogs:
You wouldn't think a seventy-five-pound German shepherd dog who is trained to chase and catch the worst of the worst criminals could be aligned with the word or principle of grace, yet Falco was graceful. When we'd go to the Children's Hospital of Orange County Oncology unit with a number of police canines, he'd put smiles on children's faces which had not smiled in months or years. He'd jump on a bed with the most delicate care to not step on a limb or tube and lay his head on a sick child's chest and, for a moment, bring love and grace to their broken world.

Police K9 Demo

www.FalcoK9Academy.com

8-Self-Control

*Like a city whose walls are broken down is a
man who lacks self-control.
Proverbs 25:28 NIV*

How many times have you done something or
reacted in a way which made you later regret your lack of
self-control? Yeah, I know, too many to count. Our sinful
natures make it easier to do the wrong thing versus the right
one. Lack of self-control in our physical and spiritual lives
lead to heartache and trouble. The least little problem or
offense causes chaos in our souls.

An undisciplined dog which is helter-skelter out of
control in your home or yard is just like the out of control

soul in a human. Gideon is a black Labrador/hound mix who needed to be around humans and get lots of stimulation. When left alone, he'd chew, destroy, and bust through the fence. Gideon also hated rain and was petrified of thunder. Even when his owner chained him to his dog house so he wouldn't break through the cat door to get inside the house or escape from the backyard, Gideon managed to pry a sheet of corrugated metal off the side of a barn to hide inside.

Gideon's owner was out of control, too. He was a drug addict and needed constant communication with humans on the phone when he wasn't doped up and sleeping. He'd hide in the barn, where he'd do drugs in secret. Unable to control his behavior, he didn't know how to control Gideon. He'd pour Tabasco sauce in Gideon's mouth for punishment or douse whatever Gideon was chewing on to get him to stop (it didn't work). He'd bite Gideon's lip, reasoning that a mother dog snaps at her puppies when they do something wrong, therefore Gideon must understand why he was getting bit (that didn't work either).

Gideon's owner eventually abandoned him in the backyard while he boarded a plane for an overseas job. Thankfully, this story has a happy ending: the owner's brother took Gideon into his home. This brother knew how to train dogs and became the leader Gideon needed. Now an old dog, Gideon is calm, happy, and obedient.

Just as there are Bible study groups, church services, mentors, and books to help you be a better follower of God, there are similar resources for dog owners. Find the system which works for your dog and the right circumstances for you to learn together as a team. Dropping the dog off with a trainer for a couple weeks or months is not learning together as a team. That's like dropping off your soul at church while your body goes elsewhere. You must be engaged and part of the process. As a dog trainer, I can train any dog with any problem to be obedient. The problem is that I become the dog's leader and the owner is still just the owner. Until the owner trains to be the leader and god to his dog, the dog's problem will continue. It takes both owner and dog to learn self-control for a happier relationship.

With love, discipline, and a proper training manual (the Bible), you can become a follower of God's Word and expectations. When the occasional failure occurs, God is there to show you the way without malice or annoyance. Even better, by putting God's Word into practice, you gain better self-control. Allowing His principles to define your boundaries gives you more patience and peace.

Paws to Pray:
Lord, I choose to do things Your way; that way, I will respond to situations with calm, confidence, and control.

Paws for Dogs:
Just like with humans, self-control in a dog sometimes needs to come from a higher power or source. Due to our sinful nature (both human's and dog's) and the lure of it's power over us, the higher power of God in you and the higher power of you in your dog is the only thing which will keep us and it from acting on sinful desires. Through consistent, loving, and respectful training, you will be your dog's god and help them maintain their self-control.

Why does my dog bark?

9-Least in the Kingdom

Few of you were wise in the world's eyes or powerful or wealthy when God called you. Instead, God chose things the world considers foolish in order to shame those who think they are wise.
- 1 Corinthians 1:26-27 NLT

One of the most unique characteristics about Jesus' teachings is His view on importance and rank. When His disciples ask who is the greatest in the Kingdom of Heaven, Jesus' responds, "The greatest in the Kingdom is whoever makes himself as humble as this child." In other words, be like the innocent kid who's too young, too short, not smart enough, and gets no respect. Later, the mother of James and John begs Jesus to give her sons the positions of greatest authority when He becomes king. Jesus replies, "Whoever among you wants to be a leader must become your servant, and whoever wants to be first must be your slave!" In other words, the highest rank is found in the lowest place.

At Falco K9 Academy, we train dogs in many different areas of detection. Whether it's narcotics, explosives, bed bugs, E. coli/salmonella, or cell phones, all these disciplines are important to the humans which the dogs serve and in many instances are the difference between life and death. While bed bugs aren't lethal (that we know of), they cause a lot of stress to a person's well being and affect their overall health. On the other hand, Cell Phone Detection Dogs can locate the phones which high level inmates use to make drug deals and arrange hits on unsuspecting victims.

Interestingly, the dogs most often chosen for these jobs come from shelters and rescues. These unwanted, undisciplined animals which are discarded and scheduled to be euthanized are often the most valuable canines available. Why is that? A detection dog must have many of the traits which cause dogs to be abandoned and abused— a dog with a lot of energy and a strong desire to hunt and be curious. A detection dog needs a strong desire to play with a toy and do anything for that toy (this often leads a dog to be mischievous and destructive if the owner is inattentive). For the same reasons one human has found a dog to be undesirable and hated, hundreds if not thousands of people find comfort and thankfulness for its existence.

God used people in the Bible and throughout history who were looked down upon by others as uneducated, sinful, and not up to religious standards. He uses unlikely people today who are considered unlovable and worthless in order to show just how great a God He is. They bring comfort, love, and leadership through their lives, their willingness to help others, and their testimonies.

I am a prime example of an unlikely person God has used. I can tell you that anyone who knew me from back in the day won't believe I've written a book about God and how to follow the example of His Son Jesus Christ. Yet here is God using an unlikely person to teach and live as an example of His Word and loving truth.

From Rahab the prostitute who helped the spies of Israel in Jericho, to the "sinful woman" who poured expensive perfume on Jesus' feet and wiped them with her hair; from simple fishermen with no religious training who became Jesus' disciples and helped spread the Good

News, to Moses and David who God took from the fields tending flocks and made them shepherds of millions of souls, God takes the "least in the Kingdom," the people we look down upon, and uses them because they are willing to be used.

Paws to Pray:
Lord, help me remember that You don't look for heroes and pedigree and status, but for humble hearts, child-like faith, and a willingness to serve.

Paws for Dogs:
The first three behaviors taught at Falco K9 Academy are non-verbal. Sit, stay, and heel are accomplished by stopping (sit), starting your walk with your right foot (stay), and starting your walk with your left foot (heel). Dogs are masters at reading body language but not at understanding the spoken word. We found that training this first makes the humans stop giving repetitive commands while the dog is forced to pay attention instead of waiting for the human to "yell" the command or take other action.

10-Temptation

*Temptation comes from our own desires, which
entice us and drag us away.
- James 1:14 NLT*

So much of the world can be a distraction from God and His glory. Because of free will, it's up to our own discernment to stay focused or distracted. Do we stay obedient or do we take a taste of the forbidden fruit—or do we eat the whole apple?

Especially when walking a dog, we must remember that their world is full of distractions (sniffing and marking on trees and bushes is essentially the "Doggy Internet." Think of how engrossing the Internet is for you and you get some idea of what going for a walk is like scent-wise for your dog). When the Bible says lusting after something or someone is sinful, the same principle applies to dogs. Handlers must understand what causes a dog to have bad thoughts and know when it is thinking bad thoughts.

A dog will often tell you what it is thinking through its body language, such as a change in position of the tail, ears, and stance, or the dog's breathing may become rapid or stop, or the fur on its neck and back will stand. Dogs are horrible at hiding their emotions. Very few dogs will strike without giving notice through their body language (pit bulls are an exception). Some dogs even wag their tails before they bite you. They are able to lie through their body language.

If you want to be a good leader for your dog and when you demand obedience and control, you must get into its mind. Read your dog and act when you *know* it is thinking bad thoughts. If you wait for it to act you are too late, for a taste or a sniff of forbidden fruit will lead to trouble.

Much of the Bible talks about loving God and Jesus and having them in our hearts and minds. If they are present there, you'll be better at avoiding those things which are not of God and His glory. Earthly things must become dim. For men, it's usually things like pornography, alcohol, hanging out with guy friends, or ogling women. For women, it might be excessive spending, spreading themselves too thin between work, kids' extracurricular activities, and church/social activities, or an obsession with body perfection.

A human handler must become a dog's focus. You need to be in your dog's heart and mind so when it is tempted to go after that Jack Russell Terrier at the park, instead it will turn to you and look in your eyes and tell you how much it loves and respects you and your presence. Or, when a pot roast is on the counter in the kitchen, it will come to you instead of "surfing the counter" and lay at your feet.

Paws to Pray
Jesus, You keep me in perfect peace when I fix my thoughts on You and not the things of this world.

Paws for Dogs:
Does your dog walk with its attention on you or does it sniff the ground and each tree, bush, or fire hydrant you come to? In order to building a loving and respectful relationship with your dog, you must create an understand with your dog that you are to

be focused on when called to do so and, when appropriate, the dog will be given the "okay" to be a dog. A healthy balance is key to this relationship.

11-Sin

But unless you repent,
you too will all perish,
– Luke 13:5 NIV

Don't you hate it when someone doesn't take responsibility for his or her actions? It's easy to blame someone else for your failures when the only thing you can honestly blame is your own sinful nature. And don't say, "The devil made me do it," because the Bible proves you a liar: "Temptation comes from our own desires, which entice us and drag us away." (James 1:14 NLT). By blaming the devil, you're not taking responsibility for yourself. It's our sinful nature which causes us to stray from what is good and right.

Dogs have a sinful nature which is why I have a successful dog training company where we teach obedience classes. Sometimes we see the same dog and human over and over because they both have sinful natures and never learn their lessons through application and consistency. Humans try to escape the stress of life through ungodly things. When a dog does this, we call it "avoidance behavior." Avoidance behavior is when a dog backs up or tries to run away when it senses a human is upset. It's not because it knows it did something wrong; it's merely reacting to the human's usual response. We've all come home to find the trash bin turned over and garbage strewn across the floor while Fido cringes in a corner. Fido isn't thinking, "I'm such a bad dog because I got into the trash when I know I'm not supposed to." Fido's merely waiting for its owner to yell and scold and drag it by the collar out the door. It's a learned response, a habit, and like all habits they can be broken and replaced with positive reinforcement.

As humans, we avoid/backup/run away from problems and situations but at some point we have to face the consequences of bad behavior. If we put them off or "avoid" them through alcohol, Internet, or sinful relationships, we are giving in to our sinful natures. Doing this for any period of time makes problems grow larger and get worse. Soon you have additional problems created by the avoidance of one problem, such as addiction, broken relationships, and wasted time.

Instead of giving in to the sin nature, we must recognize avoidance behaviors and *stop doing them*. There are three proactive steps we must take to deal with problems:

1. The first step is identifying what needs to "die" in your life so you can live. What's holding you back from being free from the issues, which plague your heart, mind, and spirit? What causes you to indulge in avoidance behaviors?

2. The next step is repenting of those things and do a complete one-eighty degree turn from them. "Repent" in Greek (*metanoia*) means "to change your mind." In Hebrew (*shuwb*) it means, "to turn back." Change your mind about how you've been living and turn away from it.

3. The last step is closely following the Lrd. In Judaism, to "do *t'shuvah*" means to turn from sin to God (Isaiah 6:10; Matthew 13:15 CJB). Read the Bible and pray daily. This is the equivalent of eating right and taking your vitamins-it makes you stronger spiritually. Fellowship with other believers who will encourage you along the right path. When the temptation arises to indulge in avoidance, turn from the temptation by embracing your fears and handing them over to God. When they're out of your hands and in His, you no longer "need" to worry about them.

The cool thing about repentance is when we repent and turn to God, not only are our sins wiped out but He refreshes us with His presence (Acts 3:19). It's just like taking a shower or bath after getting filthy—you feel clean and invigorated. Now who doesn't need that?

Paws to Pray:
Lord, I repent of not trusting You to see me through the hard times. Now I trust You to take care of me for I know I'm always in Your loving hands.

Paws for Dogs:

Is your dog training you? If your dog uses its nose to lift your arm to pet it and you comply, or if your dog goes to the cupboard where its treats are kept and barks or gives you "that look" and you respond by giving it the treat, your dog is training you. Be careful. This can snowball out of control and take leadership out of your hands.

12-Puppy Love

Love never fails.
- 1 Corinthians 13:8

It's not always easy to love people. 1 Corinthians 13:3-8 is the famous "love" passage in the Bible which outlines what real love is and does:

Love is patient, love is kind. It does not envy, it does not boast, it is not proud. It is not rude, it is not self-seeking, it is not easily angered, it keeps no record of wrongs. Love does not delight in evil but rejoices with the truth. It always protects, always trusts, always hopes, always perseveres. (NIV)

Living up to the standards of these verses is a lifelong endeavor. You can look back over your life and see instances when you weren't patient and kind but were envious, boastful, rude, self-seeking, easily angered, kept a record of wrongs, and failed to protect or trust. In fact, it's hard to get through a single day without failing to exhibit this kind of love, but it seems like dogs don't have a problem living up to part of the task. I'm sure dogs don't delight in evil (those of you with badly behaving dogs may have different opinions), but they do rejoice (especially Labradors). Dogs always seem to have hope as in they always hope they're going to find a mate while on a walk. A dog's love will always persevere when you are hurting or sad and need to be picked up; that's what makes them great for therapy. And if you allow them, they will never fail to show you affection.

Yet just like humans, all dogs have difficulty with the rest of what "love" is supposed to be:

Love is patient. The way dogs bark and carry on when you get home after being gone one minute or eight hours shows their lack of patience. It's like they're saying, "Where have you been? I missed you so much!"

Love is kind. So many dogs come to Falco K9 Academy because they're not kind. Most of the time this unkindness is pointed at strangers and potential evildoers, but isn't that the opposite of what God tells us? We need to be kind to all and show love to even our enemies. Dogs are bad at that.

It does not envy, it does not boast. Have you ever seen two dogs with one toy? Do they envy? When one gets the toy from the other dog, does it boast? Now add another toy to the scenario. No matter what, the toy one dog wants is the one the other dog has.

It is not rude, it is not self-seeking. Has a dog ever sniffed you in a private spot? I'm sure it believes it's being polite as this is a "natural," albeit self-seeking behavior, but it's rude from a human perspective.

It is not easily angered. Not all dogs become aggressive when angered, but dogs will hide or sulk. As a kid I had a black toy poodle named Baron who was easily angered and if he didn't bite you, he would sulk for days. He wouldn't even eat so he wouldn't have to come out of hiding and see you.

It keeps no record of wrongs. My brother Eddie teased Falco. He pulled his tail, called him names, and rattled his kennel. Then one day Falco took it upon himself to sort the clothing in the laundry basket, but he didn't do it by color or fabric. He sorted by Andy's stuff and Eddie's stuff and then destroyed Eddie's clothes. Later he peed right in the middle of Eddie's bed. Yes, dogs keep records of wrongs. When it comes to people they don't like or lack respect for, they will hold a grudge forever and will wait for the right moment to get back at them for their wrongs.

It always protects. Not all dogs bark at intruders. Many would open the front door if they could to let in a stranger for a chance to be petted. Although there are many police dogs which always protect, there are some which don't. If given a choice, they'd run.

Always trusts. Dogs don't always trust— that's how they became the first home alarm system. Most aggression exhibited on walks or in public occurs because a dog doesn't trust that the handler is able to protect and care for its safety and the dog takes it upon itself to take action.

Dogs and humans continually fail at mastering the many aspects of love, especially when it comes to the ones we love the most. It is with those we are closest to that we are the least patient, the most unkind, the rudest and most self-seeking, the quickest to anger, hold onto grudges the longest, and the list goes on. We react negatively to situations when we feel threatened and exhibit impatience, anger, and aggression when we don't get our way. We brag about ourselves and look out for Number One. We choose divorce instead of working to save a marriage. We walk away from friendships instead of swallowing our pride and fighting to save them. By doing so we're behaving no better than our dogs. God wants us to love others and prefer others over ourselves because it's the best way to live and brings you the most peace and joy.

First day home in Huntington Beach,
California October 31st, 1996

We don't keep 1 Corinthians 13:4–8 in mind enough when it comes to relationships. Yet if we look to our dogs as guides in the aspects of love they're good at, it's a step in the right direction.

Paws to Pray:
Lord, help me to love like You love. Amen.

Paws for Dogs:
Your dog's health and fitness is up to you. Your dog needs a healthy, "human grade" quality food. The food must be given in the exact amount which is appropriate for good health and proper weight. Free feeding is not a healthy way to feed your dog. It promotes obesity in most dogs and disables your ability to reinforce your position as the leader.

13-Language Barrier

*Then a great and powerful wind tore the
mountains apart and shattered the rocks
before the LORD, but the LORD was not in the
wind. After the wind there was
an earthquake, but the LORD was not in the
earthquake. After the earthquake came a
fire, but the LORD was not in the fire. And
after the fire came a gentle whisper.
- 1 Kings 19:11-12 NIV*

I spent years wondering where God was when bad things happened. Fact is, God spent those same years sending sign after sign that He was present in my life. He spoke to me through the actions and affection of Falco. Falco didn't need to speak English to comfort and console me during difficult times. He was so in tune with me that he sensed my sorrow and distress and allowed me to express emotions that I as a tough cop would never have dared express to a human. No wonder I loved that dog so much. Not only was Falco intelligent when it came to his job, he was intelligent and sensitive when off-duty.

Much research has been done on animal intelligence. From chimps, which use sign language and tools to ants who estimate numbers to detection dogs who sniff out odors and offenders, we should never take animals for granted. It's easy to lose patience with these creatures and subscribe their mistakes and bad behavior to being "dumb animals," but they're not dumb. There's simply a language barrier between humans and animals and it's up to us to learn their language and train them to understand ours.

If an animal could speak our language, who knows what it would say? Actually, it happened once. In Numbers 22:28 & 30, God enables a donkey to speak to its owner, Balaam the prophet. When the donkey sees an angel in the road with a drawn sword, it, being savvy when it comes to angels (especially those with swords), moves off the road and into a field. Balaam can't see the angel and gets mad at the donkey. Then the angel stands in the road where it's narrow and hedged by stone walls. Donkey, wanting to avoid the angel, pushes up against a wall, accidentally crushing Balaam's foot. Finally, the angel stands in the road where it's so narrow the donkey can't move out of the way, so it simply lays down.

In all three instances of the donkey displaying its "stupidity" (from Balaam's point of view), Balaam beats it. "What have I done to you to make you beat me these three times?" asks the donkey. "I'm your donkey, right? You've ridden me all your life, right? Have I ever treated you like this before?" Then Balaam sees the angel (who scolds him for beating the donkey) and realizes his faithful ride isn't being stubborn or stupid. It's doing what any *intelligent* creature would do *by getting out of the way*. Balaam doesn't correctly translate the donkey's language (actions) until God miraculously makes it speak.

A language barrier develops between us and God when we don't take the time to listen. He speaks through His Word, gives us nudges in our spirits, and sends signs and people to help us, but we so easily miss what He's saying. Sometimes we do hear Him but don't understand His reasoning (this happens when His plan isn't the same as ours) so we get frustrated. But God doesn't get frustrated. He's patient and works with us until we get it right, just like a good dog trainer with a dog. The dog may not understand the handler's purposes, but it learns to trust the handler.

Let's learn to trust our Handler.

Paws to Pray:
Jesus, help me to listen when You speak and to hear what others are really trying to say.

Paws for Dogs:
Watch your dog for a few days. Learn about its personality and what it looks like when it is happy, sad, curious, fearful, confident, playful, and what it looks like when it has to relieve itself. By knowing your dog's body language, you'll be able to get into its brain and anticipate bad behavior.

Why does my dog chew?

www.FalcoK9Academy.com

14-Discernment

Yes, if you will call for insight and raise your voice for discernment, if you seek it as you would silver and search for it as for hidden treasure—then you will understand the fear of ADONAI and find the knowledge of God.
- Proverbs 2:3-5 CJB

If there's one thing everyone needs more of it's discernment. Discernment to navigate through daily life, business deals, family issues—you name it, we need it. Discernment protects us from potentially dangerous situations, physically, emotionally, and financially. Discernment helps us make right decisions. We see situations in a certain light and make assumptions based on what we see, but it's discernment which enables us to see what can't be seen and get to the truth of a matter to apply correct solutions.

During Falco's career, he had to bite the suspect in close to eighty arrests. One of the most interesting arrests was one where he refrained from biting the suspect for a very discerning reason.

One night Falco and I were searching for a stolen vehicle suspect. Because it was 3 a.m., I let Falco search off leash. This also allowed Falco to search more naturally, like a wolf in the wild using his nose (his main God-given means of discernment) to hunt. He sprinted towards a parking structure under a real estate office and turned the corner out of my sight. I soon heard the usual, "Okay, I give up. I'm sorry. Please call off your dog!" What was unusual is I didn't hear the normal muffled growling when Falco had a part of the suspect's anatomy in his mouth. Instead, I heard a rhythmic barking. I thought the suspect must have jumped up on a car or was cowering behind a barrier.

As I turned the corner with gun drawn, I was shocked to see Falco standing in front of the suspect who was pressed against a wall with his hands up. The suspect was bleeding from his arms and legs and his clothing was torn.

The injuries and damage to his clothes were consistent with dog bites, but Falco's bite was more concise from years of training and usually directed toward one spot due to his ability to catch the suspect on the first bite. These bites were more defensive in their pattern. As I handcuffed the suspect, I asked him if Falco bit him. He replied, "Not this time, but when I was in that backyard he did." He pointed with his chin at a backyard just south of us, yet Falco and I hadn't gone that far. I realized the suspect had jumped in the wrong backyard and was bit by a dog protecting his family and their property.

Falco had never done this before. He was trained to do what is called "Find and Bite" to make sure a suspect can't get away. He happily did this with no hesitation, even though as a young dog in Germany he was trained in a sport called *Schutzhund*. In this sport, dogs are trained to stop and stand or sit or jump and bark inches away from the training helper but not bite him. Though Falco had this training, I was convinced he'd never do it again because "Find and Bite" is *way* more fun.

I was puzzled why he decided not to bite this felony suspect as he had done several times before and hundreds of times in training. Could he see or smell the open wounds and saliva of the other dog? Was it the fear in the man's voice which told him he had had enough? It's another mystery about dogs to which only God knows the answer.

Of course, I had to find out what kind of dog was in that backyard. I walked down the alley to the house and saw blood on the wall and on the ground. I jumped up on the wall and looked over the fence. A large Lab mix ran toward my flashlight. As if it recognized my uniform, it wagged its tail and panted happily as if asking, "How'd I do?"

He did just fine. This dog had the discernment to recognize a threat to its family and apply the Jaws of Justice, just as Falco had the discernment to recognize the suspect was no longer a threat and refrained from biting him.

Discernment teaches us when to act and when to refrain. It guards us and guides us (Proverbs 2:11). And do you know what? It's something God is eager to give us more of if we'll simply ask for it.

Paws to Pray:
Lord, make me more discerning. Amen.

Paws for Dogs:
Understand that a dog's view of the world is entirely different from ours. Don't humanize

your dog (anthropomorphize) because your dog *is not* and *never will be* human. The dog's view of the world comes first through its nose. When it uses its eyes, it's from a much lower perspective than ours. Enjoy the fact your dog is a dog and it does non-human dog things.

15-What to Do

You have already been told what is good,
What ADONAI demands of you.
– Micah 6:8 CJB

Lots of people take issue with the Bible due to evil things done, past and present, in the name of God. Others attack the Bible as being made up of fictitious stories which are supposedly not supported by historical documentation or scientific inquiry (depending on the sources used to justify or deny this position). Consequently, they disregard the Bible as irrelevant to this day and age and seek other sources of inspiration on how to best live their lives.

However, the Bible is chock-full of incredibly simplistic yet incredibly wise sayings on what is good and how to live. One of those verses is Micah 6:8:

> *He has showed you, O man, what is good. And what does the LORD require of you? To act justly and to love mercy and to walk humbly with your God. (NIV)*

Most people have a hard time doing the good stuff—acting on what is right, showing grace and fairness, and walking in humility and purity before God. Dogs have a hard time, too—even the well-trained ones. And then there are days when they get it.

Part of our job as the K9 team was to organize public relations for the police department in the form of neighborhood watch and special interest group meetings and schools assemblies. We'd talk about the K9 unit and demonstrate the dog's abilities. Once I spoke to a neighborhood watch crowd of about thirty persons near the pool area of an apartment complex with Falco off-leash. As I answered a question, a father who was standing behind the seated audience suddenly gave chase to his toddler who ran toward the pool. Falco spotted this "suspect" on the run and bolted through the audience (nearly knocking a few people to the ground) to rescue the child. By the time I realized what was going on, Falco was already more than halfway to the now frozen father who clutched his child. I yelled, "Falco, NOOOOOOO!" Falco slowed his pace but went all the way to the father and took a bite of his sweatshirt, leaving four perfect holes—his signature—as if to say, "Don't do that again." Falco returned to me and laid down at my feet, satisfied with a job well done.

I finished my speech as if nothing had happened but afterward hurried to the father. I thought for sure I'd hear the all-too familiar, "I want your badge number and name!" Instead, the man said, "Wow! That is the greatest thing I've ever seen. Your dog thought I was going to harm my son. He thought I was a kidnapper or something. That was so awesome." I shook his hand and meekly offered to pay for his damaged shirt, but he replied, "No, I'm going to keep it. That was great!"

As I sighed with relief, little did I realize that Falco had just demonstrated what it means "to act justly and love mercy and to walk humbly." By going to the rescue of the toddler, he did right; by biting the sweatshirt and not the father, he showed mercy; and by obeying my command of "NOOOOOOO!" and returning to my side, he humbled himself before his god/handler.

If only had I walked with God like that during that time, how much better would my life have been? Perhaps I still would have faced the same problems and issues, but with the right attitude, I bet there would've been a lot more peace in my life.

God doesn't make it complicated to hear Him and understand what He considers good. That's the easy part. The difficult part is living it because our sinful natures rebel against God. We want to do the wrong thing, exact revenge and punishment, and walk in pride. The dog which does that won't be much use to the agencies which need the assistance of dogs to help keep people safe. The human who does that won't be much use to God to help others and spread His Kingdom.

Paws to Pray:
God, help me to obey Your commands and do the things I know I ought to do, because at the end of the day and at the end of my life, I'll be glad I did.

Paws for Dogs:
The down command/behavior for a dog should be one of certainty. If your dog learns *down* means *down* and must be held until it is given the "free" command, you'll be able to use this command to get control of your dog

when someone is at the door or when you're
on a walk and encounter a dog which your dog
hates.

16-Days Like These

I have been very zealous for ADONAI the God of armies . . . . Now I'm the only one left, and they're after me to kill me too.
- 1 Kings 19:14 CJB

There are days when everything goes according to plan. There are days full of pleasant surprises and joy and sunshine. And then there are days when everything goes wrong. It's during those times when we need to remember God is still in control, that He is still directing our steps and isn't surprised in the least about what is happening.

The prophet Elijah had one of those days. He was involved in a showdown with the prophets of Baal and Asherah in which the entire nation of Israel watched. It was like the Superbowl of God vs god. God won and after commanding the prophets of the false gods to be put to death, Elijah prayed for it to rain (it hadn't rained for three years in Israel) and it did.

What an exciting story with a great ending, right? Wrong. Jezebel the queen sent Elijah a message saying she was going to kill him, so he headed for the hills and was ready to die because he assumed he was the only prophet of God left. In a matter of hours, Elijah went from bold victor to scared fugitive.

I had a night on patrol which started out fine but quickly fell apart. My nephew Brian joined me on a ride-a-long. This is when someone in the community rides with a police officer for a shift to see what happens while on patrol. Normally when you want to show someone how exciting the life of a cop is by taking him or her on a ride-a-long nothing happens, but with Brian, everything happened.

As we patrolled for criminal activity, we found it at a 7-11 store. While driving westbound on La Palma Avenue approaching West street I could see the clerk was yelling and waving his hands in the air while a man on the other side of the counter pointed something at him. Meanwhile, a car sat idling on curb. I instantly turned southbound on West Street from La Palma and when I pulled behind the suspicious vehicle, the brake lights came on and I knew the driver had put the car into drive. At that same moment the suspect inside the store tried to flee while the clerk struggled to hold onto him.

As I alerted area units and dispatch of my activity, the car pulled away. At the same time, the suspect in the store escaped and ran north across the parking lot. I jumped out of the car and reached back to open the back door for Falco, but the patrol car was still rolling. I hadn't come to a complete stop or shifted it into park. I jumped back in the driver's seat but it was too late. The car went up the curb and hit a small tree on the sidewalk.

Now that the car *was* stopped, I jumped out again to get Falco but the rear door was open and Falco was gone. I had unlatched the door and Falco must have pushed it open. I looked up to see Falco running across La Palma Avenue (a very busy street at 7 p.m.) about twenty-five yards behind the suspect. He had identified the suspect and went after him without my command. I turned to tell Brian to stay in the car but he was gone, too. Unbelievably, that kid was running south on West Street after the suspect vehicle.

I radioed in the additional information and that I was going into the neighborhood across from the 7-11 to look for my K9 who was chasing the suspect. I ran across La Palma and turned north onto West Street. I didn't see or hear anything as I yelled Falco's name. I listened for the typical things a suspect utters when captured by Falco the super police K9. At the same time I heard on the radio that Brian was safe and the clerk confirmed he had been robbed at gunpoint. Finally I heard, "Please help! Get him off." I ran into the courtyard of an apartment unit and saw Falco had the suspect cornered in some bushes. Because the suspect was seen with a gun, I ordered him to show me his hands. Once he did, Falco and I dragged him out. After ordering Falco to let him go I handcuffed him. That's when the smell hit me. I thought I had stepped in dog poop before realizing the odor came from the suspect.

Falco had scared the poop out of him.

Thank goodness I didn't have to transport him to jail.

While this is a humorous example of how things can go not only wrong but completely out of control, it proves my point. When life spirals out of control *from our point of view*, when things go from bad to worse, remember that the God who made the universe, who knows when each sparrow falls to the ground, is still guiding your life. Elijah experienced this. Job knew it all too well. He even said about God, "I know you can do everything, that no purpose of yours can be thwarted." (Job 42:2 CJB).

No matter what happens, God is in control. When our faith is in Him, it's never misplaced.

Oh by the way, the next day in the Orange County Register the story of this robbery talked about how a K9 handler foiled a robbery and caught 4 suspects in the process. It really should have said, "Police K9 catches armed suspect while his handler ran his patrol car into a tree and his civilian 18-year-old nephew caught the other three suspects."

Paws to Pray:
Lord, help me to keep my eyes on You and not on my circumstances.

Paws for Dogs:
Who goes out first? A dog must learn to wait for its human to exit or enter a doorway or gate opening. This shows respect and obedience. Most dogs want to bolt out of these entryways. To keep from chasing your dog around the neighborhood, build this behavior into your daily ways of operating with your dog.

17-Loss

For everything there is a season,
A time for every activity under heaven— A
time to be born and a time to die.
— Ecclesiastes 3:1-2 NLT

Losing someone we love is never easy. The Bible shares stories of families who have lost husbands, fathers, brothers, sons, daughters, and friends. Elisha lost his mentor, the prophet Elijah, when he was swept away to heaven on a fiery chariot. Jesus' disciples thought they'd lost Him—until He rose from the dead, but then forty days later He ascended to heaven, leaving the Holy Spirit as their Comforter. When David learned his best friend Jonathan died, he lamented, "How I weep for you, my brother Jonathan! Oh, how much I loved you! And your love for me was deep, deeper than the love of women." (2 Samuel 1:26 NLT).

In place of this person we are left with a gaping hole in our hearts. For some, the loss of this person means more than the loss of companionship and emotional support; it means the loss of income, home, and way of life. And it hurts, period.

Loss hurts even when you lose a pet companion. In 1996, Falco started slowing down. What used to be simple movements became difficult tasks. He acquired a sway to his walk as if he were unstable. The vet's diagnosis confirmed my fears: Falco suffered from *Spondylosis deformans*, or deterioration of the spine.

This is often caused by repeated microtrauma or repetitive pressure on joints and bones, such as running after a decoy (helper who wears bite equipment) and hitting them at high speed. Along with the brutal training of police dogs, decoys were often poorly trained and instead of smoothly catching the dogs, they would turn and run toward the dogs, creating a powerful impact. It is unnecessary and done way too often. There was never time in the eighty arrests where Falco bit a suspect where the man or woman *ever* turned toward him and caused an impact. There's no doubt that a dog needs to experience pressure in order to not be surprised on the street by a combative suspect, but at no time is it necessary for the dogs to run directly into a brick wall again and again.

As the days went by, he quickly deteriorated. This was during a horrible time in my personal life. My marriage was ending and my best friend was becoming paralyzed and was no longer able to care for himself. I didn't want to let go of Falco, who had been my emotional support for years. Even though it was clear I needed to let go, I couldn't bring myself to end his life. It got to the point Falco couldn't even walk himself outside to go to the bathroom. If my timing was off and I didn't carry him outside, he'd lie in his bed and relive himself. It was horrible.

After days of agonizing over the decision, I went downstairs to where Falco was lying in the garage in his spot. He looked at me in a way which said, "Andy, it's time. I'm ready to go." I made an appointment with his favorite vet at the Anabrook Animal Hospital in Anaheim. Before we left, I brought Falco a Double-Double cheese burger and large fries from In & Out Burger. As I hand-fed him, I think I saw a smile as he devoured the meal with gusto. Then I picked him up and put him in the backseat of the car and drove him to the vet's office.

It was the longest forty-five minutes of my life. During that time I thought about every moment of our lives together, starting with the day I was named the next K9 handler in the department and told the names and breeds of dogs who'd be available to me. I didn't need to see the other dogs once the vendor told me Falco's name. I knew a dog with that name, Falco von Aramis, would be my protector and friend.

I pulled up to the vet's office and parked. I slowly picked him up and slowly walked to the front door. I was trying to savor every moment. I wanted to remember his smell and for him to lick me just a few more times. I needed him to lick the tears from my face. He did. My friends at the office saw me coming and took me to the room where we'd spend our last moments together. I laid him on the table and sobbed as I thanked him for saving my life and for allowing me to be his handler. I apologized for the early years when I didn't know any better about how to train police dogs and thanked him for teaching me how to love and respect him and the rest of the dogs in the world.

Dr. Hendricks entered the room and asked me how I wanted to handle the procedure. As much as I thought I should be the one to give him the injection which would relieve him of his discomfort, I couldn't do it. I told Dr. Hendricks that I wanted him to do it while I laid next to Falco and held him in my arms and looked into his eyes. At that moment, eye to eye, his head on my shoulder, I felt his every breath. The look on his face was of pure love and thankfulness. And then his eyes slowly closed and his breathing stopped. "I love you, Falco," I sobbed.

Andy and Falco in Tucson, Arizona for a K9 Competition.

As hard as loss is, letting go of the person or thing afterward can be even harder. Ecclesiastes 3:4 says there is, "A time to cry and a time to laugh. A time to grieve and a time to dance." (NLT). We need to take the time to grieve and embrace painful emotions in order to move past them. If we fear being sad, then we'll carry grief with us for years because we avoid processing the feelings.

At times these strong emotions may feel overwhelming but in time they will fade. In time we will laugh and dance again—and we'll be better people for having loved a person (or dog) who made our lives better. And that isn't a loss.

Paws to Pray:
Jesus, when the pain of loss bombards me, I give it to You.

Paws for Dogs:
Did you know that forty-five minutes of exercise a day may reduce your chances of heart disease and cancer by fifty percent? Make sure you and your dog go for daily forty-five minute walks. The time with your dog may add years to your life.

18-Teamwork

The one who plants and the one who waters work together with the same purpose. And both will be rewarded for their own hard work.
- 1 Corinthians 3:8 NLT

Everyone has a part to play in building the Kingdom of God. Some have a gift for leading and teaching; others work behind the scenes doing administrative tasks. Still others are creative, using their flair for the artistic to bring glory to God. "Each one should use whatever gift he has received to serve others, faithfully administering God's grace in its various forms." (1 Peter 4:10 NIV). When everyone plays their part, the Body of Christ matures and is blessed and encouraged. It's holy teamwork in action.

When people don't do their parts or get jealous of the ones getting all the attention or get possessive of their roles, the system breaks down, problems arise, and people don't receive all God's blessing, which they could be receiving from God's Team.

Up until the time I became angry with God, my career with the Anaheim Police Department had been a storied one. I was one of the youngest police K9 handlers in the department's history; I won the Officer of the Year Award and the Distinguished Service Award (the highest award) after only five years on the force. I was on the Disney Channel for my work in an organization called Disney GOALS, helping children in the lower income areas of Anaheim through hockey. I was married and had a beautiful daughter, Courtney, who was daddy's little girl.

Courtney and K9 Titus from Orange Police Department
www.FalcoK9Academy.com

Then I began to believe I'd done all these things by myself with no help from God, so I did more to gain accolades for myself and to gain honor. It worked: I got my dream job of in-house trainer for the police K9 unit. I was on cloud nine and so proud of me.

With an ego like that, it didn't take long for discontent to set in toward my supervisors. After all, I knew more than anyone else what was good for the K9 unit. I was the one traveling around the world training police officers and K9s. I soon fell out of favor due to my arrogance and inability to work as a team member. Then I divorced my wife. Courtney and I were reduced to living with Ken Rush, a friend of mine from high school. She had a room while I slept on the couch. My life spiraled out of control. To make matters worse, Falco died. Without God and now without my dog, I had no one to listen to my whining about everyone else, no one to make me feel better with the wag of a tail or snout on my shoulder. Despite my failures, I was convinced I could do life by myself.

How wrong I was.

Have you ever seen a sled dog team? Teams of up to sixteen dogs pull a sled together in unity, each position vitally important to the success of the run. The all-important lead dog, point dogs, swing dogs, team dogs, and wheel dogs must demonstrate speed and endurance—and a willingness to know their places and get along. If they don't, their team won't win races or make it from one place to the next.

If sled dogs hadn't done their respective jobs, the 1925 serum run to Nome, Alaska (commemorated by the annual Iditarod Trail Sled Dog Race) might have ended on a tragic note.

If Falco and my other K9 partners didn't do their part in helping me patrol, I wouldn't be writing this today.

When we think we can do it all and refuse to cooperate with others, we do ourselves and everyone else a disservice. Jesus—the Son of God—worked with a team: the Twelve Disciples. Even Judas is mentioned having a specific role (group treasurer). The Early Church worked as a team (see Acts 6) with activities ranging from teaching and prayer to distributing food to widows. Seven men were prayerfully chosen for this last task to free up the Apostles to do the more spiritual tasks.

No matter how gifted a person is, they can't do everything. They always benefit from teamwork.

Paws to Pray:
Lord, help me play my part in Your Kingdom and help me allow others to play theirs, no matter what role it is.

Paws for Dogs:
Falco and I teamed up to find the worst criminals on the planet. There's something you and your dog can do together as a team which will enhance yours or someone else's life. Get on the Internet and find something which interests you and is within your dog's abilities which you can do together. It may be a sport, therapy, or service. Part of the fun will be learning this skill and then implementing it.

Bite work

19-Church

And let us not neglect our meeting together, as some people do, but encourage one another.
- Hebrews 10:25 NLT

Socializing with your dog is like being a part of a church. Church is a combination of spiritual and social interaction where its many members all have something to contribute in order to encourage one another and grow in God.

When you withdraw from this community and choose to be alone to wallow in problems, anger, self-pity, or shame, you'll be like a dog which has been left to fend for itself. It will either starve, break out of its yard to become a stray, or get hit by a vehicle or picked up by animal control and euthanized. Like that dog, you will starve from lack of fellowship, stray from God's Word and a right way of living, and fall into trouble.

When my life was speeding downhill, God used a yellow Labrador retriever puppy named McKinley to bring me one step closer to Jesus. I started Falco K9 Academy as a side business while still working on the police force. We had a pet training program along with training police and detection dogs. McKinley and his foster mother, Beth, signed up for our obedience course as a requirement of the Guide Dogs of America fostering program.

Beth was (and still is) an attractive woman who I immediately wanted to get closer to. Although I wasn't scheduled to teach this class, I added myself to the schedule and began tutoring Beth and McKinley. Soon Beth and I started dating.

Beth was a Christian. She talked a lot about her faith and church and eventually talked me into visiting her church. I'd never been to a Christian church, as I was raised a Catholic, but I liked it. The pastor, Mathew Cork at Friends Church in Yorba Linda, California spoke right to me, presenting God and Jesus in a way I could understand. But it wasn't long after leaving the sanctuary when I fell back into my world. Accountability and fellowship with Christians was not a priority.

After Beth and I married, I resisted attending church. The things which made the perfect church for me at that time were good music and a gifted speaker. Old eighties praise songs with one guitar weren't going to cut it and since I was publicly speaking on a regular basis, I *at least* had to gain some tips by watching a learned speaker. Consequently, we ended up a mega-church in South Orange County which suited my requirements. Soon the drive became a hassle and popping in for an hour on Sunday morning made forming relationships difficult.

It was then I developed an understanding for the need of fellowship with a church family and I truly began my walk with God. As a broken man who struggled with life, relationships, and faith in God and His Son, I needed a place of accountability and relationship just as I needed the dogs in my life to help get me into God's arms so that I could be saved.

You likely have many choices about which church to attend, a place where you can get fed and encouraged along with members and friends who care about you. Many dogs do not have those choices. They have been abandoned, left alone, and discarded. They don't have a church, which notices when they've gone missing. You may be the only "church" they have.

Paws to Pray:
Jesus, just like You had friends among your disciples, help me to be a friend so I may encourage others in their walks with You, and by being a friend, I know You will put people in my path who will encourage me.

Paws for Dogs:
Are you having trouble meeting new people? Your dog will help you overcome social barriers. Over eighty-three percent of dog owners who walk their dogs talk to other pet owners while they're out. Fifty percent of dog owners say they've gotten to know people in their neighborhood as a result of their dogs. Over eleven percent of dog owners took part in social or community activities as a result of their dogs.

20-Brokenness

*The sacrifice you desire is a broken spirit.
You will not reject a broken and repentant
heart, O God.
- Psalm 51:17 NLT*

Can anyone go through life without acquiring a few scars, both physical and emotional? Divorce, death, tragedy, loss, and failure leave us bruised and broken. Some people bounce back quickly; others spend years finding peace; others never bounce back. Meanwhile, we feel useless, unable to do anything for God because we hurt too badly. Some wander further from Him, never realizing that He uses whoever it takes to draw us back.

www.FalcoK9Academy.com

Beth and Montana

After dating for a few months, Beth and I broke up but she stayed on my mind. There was something about her spirit and her message, which told me, I needed God even while I was so far away from Him. I was still trying to live life on my own terms and making a mess of it and my career. Enter Montana, another yellow Labrador retriever and Beth's second foster dog from Guide Dogs of America. Montana gave me an excuse to call Beth to see if I could convince her that this broken man was worthy of her love and attention. Feigning interest in Montana, I convinced Beth to meet me for coffee. Or did God convince her in order to get me back to the person who'd be instrumental in bringing me to Him?

It worked.

On one of our dates, I took Beth on a ride-a-long (now you know why this isn't a dating manual). The last call of the night was a domestic violence call. While entering the intersection of La Palma and Lakeview, a man ran a red light and we collided. I was knocked unconscious from the impact while Beth broke her hand. The concussion I suffered from the crash, compounded by concussions from playing football, pole-vaulting, and hockey, eventually retired me from my twenty year career in law enforcement.

Although I fought retirement, it led me to what was becoming my personal salvation—working with dogs. Falco K9 Academy became my full time focus. Once again God put dogs in my life as an example of His greatness and to lead me to Him and His grace.

God does not give up on us.
You must not give up on your dog.

www.FalcoK9Academy.com

Have faith and confidence in both yourself and the dog's ability to learn. Hundreds and thousands of dogs are euthanized with the excuse they're un-trainable and damaged beyond repair. As a trainer, I've seen that very few dogs are broken beyond repair. Just as Jesus sought out the broken and showed them grace, love, and respect, you as a leader need to do the same for your dog. With the right guidance, they have a lot to offer.

Just as Jesus seeks out you and me—the broken— and shows us grace, love, and respect, with His guidance we have a lot to offer.

It starts with a broken spirit and repentant heart.

Paws to Pray:
Jesus, even when I'm broken, use me to draw others to You.

Paws for Dogs:
Consider training and certifying your dog for therapy service. If your dog is social and likes being around new environments you may be able to bring joy into someone else's life. Anecdotal evidence demonstrates children with autism are often more able to connect with dogs than with people. Kids with dogs may be calmer, have better concentration, and improved social interactions.

21-Name Change

They will see his face, and his
name will be on their foreheads.
- Revelation 22:4 NIV

The New Testament makes it loud and clear that following Jesus means putting Him first and all else second. He warns in Matthew 10:35-39 that He comes to turn family member against family member and that a man's enemies will be his own household. Jesus adds anyone who loves his family more than Him isn't worthy of Him, but promises that anyone who loses his life for His sake will find it. Those are hard words yet many across the globe and time have faced rejection from family because of their decision to follow Jesus.

I faced a similar situation from my family, not because of faith in Christ (I wasn't a believer yet), but because of Beth. As we became serious, my immediate family became resentful of her as they realized my divorce from my ex-wife was a reality. It wasn't until I informed them I was bringing Beth to our family Christmas gathering did I see how grim the situation was. They had invited my ex-wife and "didn't think it would be a good idea if I brought Beth." I insisted if Beth wasn't allowed to come then I wasn't coming either.

Without God in my life, I was slow to forgive, resentful, and not respectful of their decision. I tried every way I could think of to show them they were wrong, but my mom, dad, two sisters, and brother were simply in love with my ex-wife and didn't want to believe we couldn't work it out. If they would have been to the *eight* different therapists and counselors and mediation sessions maybe they would have understood. But they didn't. They loved us together and somehow thought the divorce was my decision and Beth was keeping us from getting back together.

When planning our wedding, I invited my family in one last effort to save our relationship. They refused to come. Beth told me she couldn't respect the name of people who shunned her, but because of her love for me she wanted to take my name, so she asked if she could take the last name Falco.

At the time I was a detective in the Sex Crimes Unit, investigating the worst crimes in the community and taking predators off the streets and putting them behind bars. You haven't lived until you've made a child molester or rapist's day miserable by putting him in prison or back in prison. I was also doing a lot of work in the public eye. I taught K9 systems and techniques around the world; I worked in the Disney GOALS program and was on the Disney Channel; I was also President of the Orange County Police Canine Association. I was constantly in the newspaper and on TV and radio.

Consequently, I became concerned for my five-year-old daughter's safety. I felt the need for a work identity and a private identity for protection. That's when I realized many people thought my last name was 'Falco' due to the name of my business, Falco K9 Academy. Even Beth thought my last name was Falco until she joined me on a ride-a-long (honestly, I did take her on non-patrol dates) and saw my name tag and true last name. So here was another opportunity for Falco to protect me and my daughter. I decided for public purposes I would use Falco as my last name to confuse anyone wanting retribution.

Since it was an honorable name and the name Beth grew to love, I agreed with her request. I later added Falco to my last name. I was starting a new life and my birth family chose not be a part of it, while my in-laws embraced me and all my flaws with open arms. I have since forgiven my family and have told them so, yet to this day, after many invitations, they refuse to meet Beth and our beautiful children.

When your family rejects you because of Jesus, remember that Jesus adopts you into His family. It's not your family surname or an alias which identifies you as one of His children, but His name. In *His* name you will do *His* works and expand *His* kingdom. And in Eternity, it gets even better:

> To him who overcomes, I will give some of the hidden manna. I will also give him a white stone with a new name written on it, known only to him who receives it. (Revelation 2:17 NIV)

Paws to Pray:
Jesus, it's Your name and not mine that counts in this world and the world to come. Amen.

Paws for Dogs:

A dog's name should be respectful, loving, and something you're proud of. It can remind you of someone you respect or is the best at something (Gretsky); or a place you love to visit (Montana); or a name of power and honor (Falco) which inspires you. You'll say this name often and will want to bring about positive feelings about your dog even when they are doing something wrong, so refrain from giving them a negative name or nickname like "Dumb Dog" or "Worthless." What you repeat will become true in your heart and mind, so be respectful, loving, and proud of your dog and its name.

22-Higher Intelligence

*His works are perfect, and all his
ways are just. A faithful God who
does no wrong, upright and just is he.
- Deuteronomy 32:4 NIV*

God and His creation are so great and vast and complex that there's no way we can ever know everything about both. "As the heavens are higher than the earth, so are my ways higher than your ways and my thoughts than your thoughts" (Isaiah 55:9). When we can't comprehend the ins and outs of how something works or when we don't understand His plan and purpose for us or others, we can still trust Him. He knows what He's doing.

There are many things about dogs, which are amazing. I don't completely understand their hows and whys and I've worked with them for almost thirty years. I've studied with great trainers and scientists and still can't tell you how a dog's olfactory system enables them to find a particle of odor so minute that you must look under a microscope to see it. That same substance can be in a fifty gallon drum of water and the dog can still detect it. Then again, do I need to understand it or should I simply trust that dogs are using their God-given abilities?

When Beth and I got married, only God knew why. We were complete opposites. It was clear we didn't have the same view on intimacy. She didn't like my drinking or how I purchased on a whim without thought of need over desire or how I didn't organize my day. I had spontaneity and get up and go; Beth was a planner. I was an early riser *and* a night person; she was neither. And of course I had to go to church to please her. It also didn't take long for the relationship between my daughter Courtney and Beth to sour. But in spite of it all, God brought us together and gave us three beautiful children. It makes no sense and yet amazingly we are still married today.

What was God's purpose in it all? Hindsight being twenty-twenty, I know now Beth, who at the time was the most unlikely of wife choices because of our obvious differences, was the perfect choice and by God's grace the *only* choice. If I had married any other woman I wouldn't have found God's hand (through Beth) leading me to His Word. The messages I heard at Friends Church Yorba Linda and at Mariner's Church reached my heart at the right time using the right person. Beth's persistence and strength in times of stress and conflict made me stronger because she always chose God as she looked forward and followed Him while I was looking back and wondering where He was. Beth never gave up on her desire to lead me to Him.

We should trust God even when we don't understand His purpose (which is a lot of the time). Like the scripture verse says at the beginning of this chapter, "His works are *perfect*, and *all* his ways are just. A faithful God *who does no wrong.*" You can't go wrong with that.

Paws to Pray:
God, I only see things from my point of view. Help me to trust You more because You see the bigger picture.

Paws for Dogs:
In a world of amazing advances in technology, there's no more amazing machine than the olfactory system of a dog. No one

has been able to replicate the power of a dog's nose. It has the ability to separate numerous odors and detect microscopic substances emitted by an odor. Only a Higher Intelligence is capable of creating such a powerful machine. This is just one example of God's power.

23-Love & Respect

Respect everyone, and love your Christian brothers and sisters. Fear God, and respect the king.
- 1 Peter 2:17 NLT

Love and Respect are taught in the Bible as important actions of anyone who wants a relationship with God and His Son. You must have both. A love-only relationship is an infatuation without respect for the other person's feelings, likes and dislikes, position in the relationship, and space. A respect-only relationship is often based on fear or distrust and is not of the soul and love receptors of your brain. A love and respect relationship is perfect. It is of the mind, heart and soul.

I teach dog owners in training class they must have both the love and respect of their dog. It makes you and your dog conscious of what the other wants and desires even if they aren't with you. After the first time I taught this, I thought about my relationship with my wife Beth. Did I love and respect her and show her that? The answer was an astounding no. My love was fleeting and I showed virtually no respect. Sure, we had three kids together and I loved her family. I wasn't abusive or hateful, just distant. So there I was teaching hundreds of people about love and respect and I didn't even show my wife and God love and respect. I had to search through my memories back to my days with Falco to remember what it was like to actually have love and respect for something. I loved this dog with all my heart and soul and he loved me. He loved and respected me so much that he put himself between a gunman and me to save my life, while I loved and respected him so much that I held him in my arms when he took his last breath.

Once again, a dog helped bring me closer to God. I need to love and respect Beth and Jesus with the respect I had for Falco. Just as Falco and I were partners, I must honor and cherish Beth as a partner in marriage and as the mother of my children. I must honor and obey Jesus as my leader/handler as He uses me in advancing His kingdom.

The same goes for you and your dog. Whether it's in daily life or on a walk, there must be love and respect between you and your dog. An example of this is when you go for a walk and your dog pulls you to every tree or bush to sniff what another dog has left behind or to chase a child who's skateboarding. Chasing that kid shows the dog has more love for the chase than for you. A dog who is taught to love and respect its handler knows that leaving you to examine the base of a tree against your wishes is disrespectful. To have its respect, you must forgive (but not forget) the instant you see compliance and respect for your authority.

At Falco K9 Academy, we teach a system called "Human Training For Your Dog." This training makes humans more responsible for training their dogs out of respect and love. One of the reasons our method works so well is because the dogs and handlers work hard for the rewards to be gained for being correct (i.e they learn love and respect because of positive reinforcement) as opposed to working to avoid discomfort, punishment, or those things which can be lost for being wrong.

The result is service dogs which are hard working and reliable. The handlers also enjoy the training which is above and beyond what they might have received at another training facility. A mutual love and respect develops between dog and human.

As followers, we show our love of God by remembering there is only one God. If we pray to false gods, we show God we do not love Him. If we don't love our wives like Jesus loves His Church and become leaders in our homes and families, we show a lack of respect for Jesus and His teachings. We can't say one thing and do another and still maintain credibility as a Christian or worker or spouse or parent. We must love and respect God and others enough to pair actions with words.

Paws to Pray:
Father, help me show love and respect to everyone I meet today, both the two-legged and four-legged.

Paws for Dogs:
Does your dog respect *and* love you? Be aware of how you and your family interact with your dog. It's extremely important it doesn't get love and attention without first showing you respect. It must believe all which is good comes through you *after* respect is shown. On the flip side, demanding respect without showing love is no way to treat a dog. Look at your relationship and see where you need to balance the loving with the respectful.

Love and Respect

24-Leader of the Pack

*The Son can do nothing by himself;
he can do only what he sees his
Father doing, because whatever the
Father does the Son also does.
– John 5:19 NIV*

Many people struggle to be outstanding leaders and examples. More than at any other time in history can this be said about husbands and fathers. Many will say it is epidemic. The concept of leadership smacked me in the face one day in the form of a photo posted on Facebook. A picture was tagged of me holding a bottle of beer in one hand and a plastic cup of beer in the other. My belly protruded and I wore a stupid grin. The first thing I thought when I saw it was, "That's how my kids and wife see me." My daughters will look for a man in the image of their father—is that who I want them to find? My sons look to me as a role model—is that how I want them to act?

There is great value and payoff in leading by example *the right way*. This is seen clearly in dog training, but the same principles apply to leading humans.

As a trainer of dogs:

- I demand love and respect from every dog from the moment we meet. I set the rules and expectations of our relationship. Some dogs will resist at first but they eventually respond to my expectations.

- I am consistent and always fair. I look at each dog individually for its strengths and weaknesses. Then I work within those parameters while challenging it to overcome its weaknesses and building upon its strengths.

- I am there to guide the dogs during times of confusion, fear, lack of knowledge, and lack of confidence. I encourage them when they show even a slight improvement in any area of weakness and I reward and praise them to show how happy I am with their improvement.

- In times of failure I am responsive and decisive in correction or discipline. The level of discipline is equal to the violation.

- The moment a dog shows submission or understanding that it is wrong, I am quick to forgive and move on. I don't hold a grudge. I don't berate or make it suffer.

- My expectations are high and I encourage the dog to be better than it ever has been before. Even if it fears failure, I am always there to catch it if it falls.

- I understand their weaknesses and limitations. If a dog is simply not created to perform a specific task, there's always something else it can do and perform at an acceptable or high level.

- I lead by example or I find a dog who is a leader and allow it to lead by example. Dogs learn from other dogs. It's important that the leader is a positive role model and example.

It's not always easy being a good leader and good example, especially when we fear offending people or not being liked. Yet it's our responsibility to maintain our position as Alpha dog in our personal wolf packs. Without the Alpha playing its part, all other positions—Beta (second in command, the sergeant who enforces orders), Subordinates (the "clowns" who try to diffuse tense situations) and Omegas (lowest rank who are noisy to make enemies think the pack is bigger than it is)—become blurred and chaos ensues.

I see the positive effects these leadership principles have on every dog which comes through our doors at Falco K9 Academy. But in my home I regularly hold a grudge against my wife; I don't lead by example for my children and I'm often not there during times of confusion or fear and then ridicule or scoff at their inability. It's the same in business. When it's necessary for me to discipline or correct employees, I'm slow and sometimes absent. Sometimes I don't lead at all and instead act as an equal or follower. I don't lead by example and I don't have high expectations of my employees and accept mediocrity.

By staying God focused and on His expectations, we become by default outstanding leaders in our homes, businesses and churches. How do we know what His expectations are? We read the Bible and spend time in prayer. We as *followers* look to God and Jesus as the greatest examples of *leaders*.

Paws to Pray:
Lord, help me to follow Your lead. Amen.

Paws for Dogs:
Less than one percent of all dogs are capable of being trained to save lives and locate hidden substances as police K9 or detection dogs. This requires me to be able

to identify the leader of the pack. This dog must be strong, confident, courageous, and have an enormous amount of desire to do the job. On top of this, it must be trainable and intelligent.

What training technique?

25-Dying to Live

If any of you wants to be my follower, you must turn from your selfish ways, take up your cross, and follow me. - Mark 8:34 NLT

Recently, Lead Pastor Mathew Cork at Yorba Linda Friends Church (my church), instructed the congregation to ask themselves two questions:

1. What do I need to die to in order that I may live?
2. Am I following God or am I expecting Him to follow me?

We all can name something which hinders our walk with the Lord, but the thought that maybe we aren't really following God but instead are expecting God to follow us is a shocker. For all my life I expected God to follow me. When I asked, "Where are you God?" what I was really asking was, "Why aren't You following me?"

When you take a dog for a walk on a leash, usually one of two things happens:

a. You are in control and the dog walks beside you in a calm and happy manner. It has been trained to not tug on the leash or drag you to every scent marking left by other animals. It follows your pace and stops and sits when you tell it to.

b. The dog is in control and drags you down the path in a wild and capricious manner.

No matter how hard you pull on the leash, it strains harder against you to the point of choking itself, all to gratify its desires. You follow its pace and by the end of the walk are exhausted from the struggle and have strained arm and shoulder muscles.

Which are you? The dog who "dies" to its own ambitions, follows its Handler, respects the lead (the Holy Spirit's guidance) and obeys His commands (the Bible) for a safe and fulfilling walk, or are you the dog who runs here and there, fights the leash, and ignores your Handler because you want to be in control?

www.FalcoK9Academy.com

While writing this book, I realized there is a lot of "me" which needs to die so I may live, and to do that I need to truly follow God's word. Up until now I thought being good was good enough. But there's lots of "good works" done in the Church and ministries formed in the name of God, which He never ordained. They are man's ideas, not God's.

> Not everyone who says to me, 'Lord, Lord,' will enter the kingdom of heaven, but only he who does the will of my Father who is in heaven. Many will say to me on that day, 'Lord, Lord, did we not prophesy in your name, and in your name drive out demons and perform many miracles?' Then I will tell them plainly, 'I never knew you. Away from me, you evildoers!' (Matthew 7:21-23 NIV)

While I was doing good things and telling others how they can walk closer to the Lord, I hadn't fully committed myself to God. Sure, I had accepted Jesus Christ as my Lord and Savior and dedicated my life to Him and was doing what I thought was my best to live by His word, yet I never died to myself so I could live for Him.

All along God was asking me, "Where are you, Andy? I've been talking to you and I've been waiting for you. You can see Me if you just open your eyes. Until now you have chosen yourself over Me." Like an untrained dog which comes to Falco K9 Academy, I've been focused on me and what I want. Now it's time to focus on my Handler. Now it's time to live for Him and He'll train me for whatever duty He deems fit:

> *I will guide you along the best pathway for your life. I will advise you and watch over you. Do not be like a senseless horse or mule that needs a bit and bridle to keep it under control. (Psalm 32:8-9 NLT*

> *He trains my hands for war and gives my fingers skill for battle. (Psalm 144:1 NLT)*

What do you need to die to so you may live and follow God?

Paws to Pray:
Father, help me remember when I lose my life for You, I end up finding the best life of all.

Paws for Dogs:
As human beings with sinful natures there are some aspects of our lives, which must die if we're going to live in a way which pleases God and is in line with the teachings of Jesus Christ. For a dog to live in our world without disrupting it or causing problems, there are traits or behaviors which must die through proper training. Don't forget to show your dog the

same grace, love, and respect which the Lord shows you when you struggle and fail. Your dog needs all the encouragement it can get.

The Ten Commandments for Dog Owners

1. Thou shalt love and respect thy dog no matter when or where.

2. Thou shalt be clear, concise, and consistent with thy dog.

3. Speak with confidence and sincerity (thou shalt not yell).

4. Remember thy dog sees two feet off the ground or lower and uses its nose before sight.

5. Honor thy dog's dogginess—let it run, mark territory, play, and lay around doing nothing.

6. Thou shalt provide thy dog with proper nutrition and exercise.

7. Spend quality time with thy dog because a bored and lonely dog works all kinds of mischief.

8. Thou shalt listen to thy dog's bark and body language.

9. Thou shalt expect the same behavior from thy dog in public as in private.

10. Thou shalt have fun with thy dog always.

For more information on Andy Falco Jimenez or to contact him for speaking engagements or dog training sessions, email him at

andy@falcok9academy.com

or contact

Falco K9 Academy
615 N. Berry St. Suite F
Brea, CA 92821
714-990-9010
http://www.falcok9academy.com

http://www.WalkingWithGodAndADog.com

Check out Andy and the Falco team on YouTube at
http://www.youtube.com/user/falco143

About the Author

Andy is the President of Falco Enterprises, Inc. a company specializing in the training of humans and their dogs. The company additionally supports these customers with products and services. Andy is also the Training Director of Falco K9 Academy. Andy worked as a Police K9 handler from 1989 to 1996 for the Anaheim Police Department in California. During this period Andy became passionate about Police K9 training and dog training in general. After traveling throughout North America and Europe seeking dog training and behavior knowledge, Andy developed Falco K9 Academy in 1995. Andy was then named the police department's first in-house trainer for the K9 Unit. Andy retired from the department in 2005 to concentrate on Falco Enterprises, Inc.

About the Editor

Victoria Kovacs has written professionally since 1997. She is the author of *How to Spot a Wizard in London*, *Little Bible Heroes* series, and ghostwrites and edits children's stories, fiction, and non-fiction works, including a novel which hit #5 on the Amazon Top 100 Free Download Best Seller list. Victoria is Head Scriptwriter for Marvel Production Group and boasts a television series in her repertoire along with hundreds of scripts and screenplays. Her ability to perfectly capture a client's voice puts her

writing skills in high demand. She can be
reached at themagnificentpen@gmail.com.